REG CRIBB is a multi-award-winning writer for the stage and screen. His original plays include: *The Damned* (2012, winner of the NSW Premier's Literary Award); *The Haunting of Daniel Gartrell* (2012); *Unaustralia* (2012); *Boundary Street* (2011, winner of the Rodney Seaborn award); *Krakouer* (2010) *Uncle Vanya*; *Ruby's Last Dollar* (2005, nominated for the Victorian Premier's Literary Award); *The Chatroom* (2004, shortlisted for the Patrick White Playwright's Award); *The Return* (2001); and *Last Cab to Darwin* (2003, winner of the Patrick White Playwright's Award, the Queensland Premier's Literary Award, the WA Equity Award for Best New Play, the WA Premier's Literary Award and the WA Premier's Prize Award for Overall Literature, making history as the first play to win this award). He co-wrote the one-man play *Gulpilil* with David Gulpilil (2004).

Reg's screen credits include adaptations of *Last Cab to Darwin* (winner of an AACTA for Best Adapted Screenplay, nominated for an AWGIE for Best Adapted Feature), *The Return* (renamed *Last Train to Freo*) and *Ruby's Last Dollar*; and the true-crime screenplay *The Great Mint Swindle*. Reg co-wrote *Bran Nue Dae*, for which he was nominated for an AFI award.

THE RETURN

Reg Cribb

Currency Press,
Sydney

CURRENCY PLAYS

The Return first published in 2003
by Currency Press Pty Ltd,
PO Box 2287, Strawberry Hills, NSW, 2012, Australia
enquiries@currency.com.au
www.currency.com.au

Reprinted 2012, 2013, 2014, 2015 (twice), 2017, 2018, 2020, 2021, 2022

Copyright © Reg Cribb, 2003.

COPYING FOR EDUCATIONAL PURPOSES

The Australian *Copyright Act 1968* (Act) allows a maximum of one chapter or 10% of this book, whichever is the greater, to be copied by any educational institution for its educational purposes provided that that educational institution (or the body that administers it) has given a remuneration notice to Copyright Agency (CA) under the Act.

For details of the CA licence for educational institutions contact CA, 12/66 Goulburn Street, Sydney, NSW, 2000; tel: within Australia 1800 066 844 toll free; outside Australia 61 2 9394 7600; fax: 61 2 9394 7601; email: memberservices@copyright.com.au.

COPYING FOR OTHER PURPOSES

Except as permitted under the Act, for example a fair dealing for the purposes of study, research, criticism or review, no part of this book may be reproduced, stored in a retrieval system, or transmitted in any form or by any means without prior written permission. All inquiries should be made to the publisher at the address above.

Any performance or public reading of *The Return* is forbidden unless a licence has been received from the author or the author's agent. The purchase of this book in no way gives the purchaser the right to perform the play in public, whether by means of a staged production or a reading. All applications for public performance should be addressed to the playwright c/- Yellow Creative Management, 1/348 Darling Street Balmain, NSW 2041; tel: +61 2 8090 4421; email: contact@yellowcreativemanagement.com.

In accordance with the requirement of the Australian Media, Entertainment & Arts Alliance, Currency Press has made every effort to identify, and gain permission of, the artists who appear in the photographs which illustrate these plays.

NATIONAL LIBRARY OF AUSTRALIA CIP DATA

    Cribb, Reg.
      The return.
      ISBN 0 86819 692 4.
      I. Title.
    A822.4

Typeset by Dean Nottle
Cover design by Kate Florance.
Front cover shows Grant Bowler as Steve and Kirsty Hillhouse as Lisa. Back cover shows Tim Michin as the Writer and Grant Bowler as Steve. Photos from the 2002 Perth Theatre Company production. (Photographer: Jon Green)

Currency Press acknowledges the Traditional Owners of the Country on which we live and work. We pay our respects to all Aboriginal and Torres Strait Islander Elders, past and present.

Contents

for Alan

Introduction

Jeremy Sims

The Return marked the beginning of a new phase of collaboration between Reg and myself. Up to that point we had been fellow aspirants auditioning for NIDA in the baking heat of a Perth summer day, then fellow students of said institution, then good friends, and eventually founding members of Pork Chop Productions.

In those days Reg offered left-field acting solutions and a round of Guinness to the creative process that spawned our original productions of *Rosencrantz and Guildenstern are Dead* and *The Players* (a mime cabaret!). We had no idea there was a playwright hidden inside and, after reading a first draft of *Night of the Sea Monkey*, his first play, I for one was none the wiser. In hindsight, the stories he told about growing up in Western Australia, the 1975 Grand Final that West Perth won, and yelling abuse at Archie Duda with his uncles at East Perth Oval should have given us a clue.

Still, I have a policy of producing plays written from within the tribe and, since it wasn't too expensive to put on a co-op at the Old Fitz, we thought we'd let Reg get this writing thing out of his system. The result was exceedingly silly, occasionally hilarious, but generally awful. Unfortunately two mutual friends stole the evening with fifteen minutes of stand-up that we were obliged to have in the show in order to facilitate an interval and a modicum of profit over the bar!

Which brings us to *The Return*. I fully expected not to see another word in print from Reg after *Sea Monkey*, but a few things in his life conspired to make him think a little deeper about the whole shooting match, and after going back to Perth to grieve the death of his brother something opened up inside him—or perhaps let go—and he started writing again. *The Return* is what came out.

Credit must go to Ros Horin and the readers at Griffin who first recognized *The Return* and included it in their season of shorts. The finished work was greatly shaped during rehearsal, as was the reworked central storyline of the motives for revenge. A great deal of credit must also go to the original cast who, apart from Steve, had multiple roles to play on the evening, and it was probably a blessing that these roles were interpreted for the first time by character actors rather than 'typecast' performers. Andrea Moor's journey from Middle-Class Prude to Vamp to Maureen was particularly astounding.

Many thanks to Steve Le Marquand for creating Steve with me. He knew instinctively what Reg and I were thinking for this astonishing character. In fact, during auditions held at the Griffin, he was wandering by in bare feet and a flannie, smoking a Winnie Blue as I stood outside. He fixed me with his stare, flicked away the ciggie and asked if 'I had any fuckin' idea where the theatre was'. I told him not to bother looking as I was the director and he had just been cast.

I don't want to talk too much about what the play is about, or what it might mean. That is for you to discover. But since I am about to begin rehearsals with Pork Chop Productions of Reg's new play, *Last Cab to Darwin*, I can report that Reg continues to develop his talent for true Australian dialogue along with his instinctive feel for the 'broken' or lost idealism of modern Australia. Enjoy.

Perth
March 2003

Writer's Note

Reg Cribb

The Return was triggered by an incident that I witnessed on a suburban train. In front of a handful of commuters, two bitter, disenfranchised young men psychologically tortured a young female law student. Not one hand was laid on her, but she was visibly shaken by the incident. Apart from the claustrophobic confines of a train carriage being the perfect setting for an intense drama, the incident seemed to embody a lot of the frustration being felt in Australia today. A whole generation of young men are just hanging onto their relevance in society by their fingertips. But they are poised to fall off the edge. Drugs, mandatory sentencing, suburban alienation, the rapid acceleration and pressures of globalisation, and the absence of strong male role models are factors that have conspired to create this situation. We are losing our young men, not to war, but to an insidious battleground of the inner psyche. And women, more often than not, become the battle-scarred victims. I hope we can recognize and identify with the characters in *The Return*. We live with them, travel and work with them. They all swing by degrees between lovable and loathsome. The only thing I ask is that we not judge them.

Perth
March 2003

The Return was first produced by Griffin Theatre Company, in association with Riverina Theatre Company, at the SBW Stables Theatre, Sydney, on 16 March 2001, with the following cast:

STEVE	Steve Le Marquand
TREV	Brett Stiller
LISA	Rebecca Massey
MAUREEN	Andrea Moor
WRITER	Raj Ryan

Director, Jeremy Sims
Set Designer, Ralph Myers

CHARACTERS

STEVE, ex-con, early-mid 40s
TREV, ex-con, early 20s
LISA, university student, middle-class, mid 20s
MAUREEN, suburban housewife, late 40s
WRITER, male, middle-class, early 30s

VOICEOVER: I know this place. This is the place I was born in. The place I grew up in. The place with a hundred sun-drenched horizons to run into. The smell of it would crackle in my nostrils. Long ago, when summer couldn't kill you, I would peel the burnt skin off my body and throw it into the wind like an offering. I never cared what was happening in the rest of the world. I never cared what was happening in the rest of Australia. This was the luckiest place in the universe. You just... knew it.

I've been away for a long time. A long time. But now I'm home. It's strange the things that bring you back home. Things that you thought could never happen. Not in this town anyway.

Something's really changed here. Everything's... darker and people are scared now. Or maybe nothing's changed. Maybe I'm just older...

Heavy jarring industrial grunge music starts up. Doors slide open and two men stride onto the set. It is a suburban train carriage. Functional and soulless. The men have a dangerous, world-weary edginess about them. TREV *has a gaunt face and short spiky hair and* STEVE *has long hair tied in a ponytail. He is the most striking of the two, but also the most imposing.*

They appear to be moving in slow motion but then start to merge with the jarring rhythms of the music until they are punching and kicking the air in time with it, like a distorted war dance. The music ceases abruptly and there is a brief blackout.

When the lights come back up, we see them seated opposite each other staring impassively into each other's eyes. Some muzak-style classical music is coming over the loudspeakers. It clashes absurdly with their whole demeanour.

Nothing happens for a good minute, then the thug with the spiked hair slowly picks up a pretend violin. He launches into miming the concerto on the violin. He throws himself body and soul into the performance, moving and swaying with the concerto. At the climactic moment, he stands and begins smashing his air violin on the ground like Pete Townshend, complete with rock star arm windmills. Exhausted, he slumps back onto the seat and wipes his brow like a great artist.

The lights have been dimmed all this time and the music has been heightened. Just as abruptly, the lights come up fully and the music level lowers. They are in their original seated positions.

STEVE: Where's that fuckin' smell comin' from?

TREV: What? I can't smell a thing.

STEVE: You've trod on dog shit.

TREV: No I haven't.

STEVE: Check ya shoes.

> *He checks them.*

Under ya fuckin' shoes.

TREV: No. Check your own.

STEVE: Will ya just check the bottom of your shoes?

TREV: Nup.

STEVE: Check 'em. [*Pause.*] Check 'em. *Check 'em!*

> *They go into a cat and mouse routine. Eventually* STEVE *overpowers* TREV *and checks the bottom of each shoe separately.*

Sorry.

TREV: Not much dog shit around Midland anymore.

STEVE: No.

TREV: The locals are pretty good at pickin' up after their dogs now.

STEVE: Yeah.

TREV: Not much dog shit around Perth anymore really.

STEVE: No. Not like the old days.

> *Pause.*

TREV: Yeah, those were the days

STEVE: Shut up.

ANNOUNCEMENT: *[voice-over] Next station: West Midland.*

TREV: Notice the way she emphasises *West* Midland. It makes her sound quite… ah… what's the word… personable. 'Cause we know we're already in Midland, but she let's us know that we're on the west side *of* Midland. It makes ya feel like… it's okay… we're all in this together, folks.

STEVE *just looks at him.*

STEVE: This is gonna be a long trip.

ANNOUNCEMENT: [voice-over] Doors closing.

TREV: Did ya bring the smokes?

STEVE: Can't smoke on the train, mate.

TREV: Just checkin'.

STEVE: 'Course I did. Have I ever forgotten? Do I ever forget anything?

TREV: Dunno. Do ya?

STEVE: Sometimes I forget how stupid you are.

TREV: Gee, I'm touched. [*He glances around the carriage.*] Fuck! This music is killin' me. I mean, what is this… ah… *Reader's Digest* Twenty Most Annoying Classic Hits? [*He stands up.*] Where the fuck is it comin' from?

STEVE: Siddown! Just ignore it like I do. It's just an experiment. It'll be gone in a month.

TREV: Yeah, well I feel like a fuckin' lab rat.

STEVE: That's 'cause it's for people like you.

TREV: And you.

STEVE: Don't drag me into your compost heap, mate. I actually like some classical music.

TREV: Yeah? Which ones?

STEVE: Whadda ya mean?

TREV: Which songs do ya like specifically?

STEVE: They're not songs. They're orchestral pieces. This is Beethoven. 'Moonlight Sonata'. They're movements.

TREV: Yeah, well I'd like to do a movement on that bloody speaker. If I could find the fuckin' thing!

STEVE: Anything in the job pages today?

TREV: Yep.

STEVE: What?

TREV: Jobs.

STEVE: What jobs?

TREV: Lottsa jobs that we're not qualified for.

STEVE: What… all of 'em?

He doesn't answer.

I'll look tomorrow.

TREV: Don't bother. I got a plan.

STEVE: A plan.

TREV: Yeah. It's gonna make me a millionaire.

STEVE: Is that right?

TREV: I haven't told ya about my 'Spot the Bum' calendar, have I? Very hush-hush.

STEVE: Your 'Spot the Bum' calendar?

TREV: Oh, yeah. It's brilliant. And simple. It's brilliant because it's simple.

STEVE: Go on.

TREV: Well… it's a calendar. And every month has a different photo above it. And each photo is of a huge famous public gathering.

STEVE: Whadda ya mean… gathering?

TREV: You know, like… ah… like thousands of people in Arabia bowing to Mecca or… um… an Easter crowd at the Vatican listening to the Pope… you know?

STEVE: Yeah.

TREV: Well… in every photo, there's one person in the crowd with their daks down and their bum hangin' out! Whadda ya reckon?

STEVE: It's brilliant, Trev.

TREV: I mean people would buy it just to try and spot the guy with the browneye. It can't fail.

STEVE: So, ah… were you just gonna jetset around yourself and set up these photos or were ya gonna hire National Geographic?

TREV *just stares at him.*

Or maybe you could just… airbrush their bums in.

TREV: Maybe.

STEVE: You could even have your own website.

TREV: Yeah.

STEVE: www.spotthebum.com.

TREV: Don't… don't piss on my fire, mate.

STEVE: Or… or how 'bout… www.spotthedate.com.

TREV: You can shut up now.

STEVE: I got it! www.spotthedateunderthedate…

TREV: Finished?

STEVE: Dot.

TREV: Have ya?

STEVE: Com. Ya wanna be a shaker and a mover, don't ya? I'm just lookin' out for your well-being.

ANNOUNCEMENT: *[voice-over] Next station: Guildford.*

TREV: Why don't we go away somewhere?

STEVE: Away where?

TREV: I dunno. Somewhere.

STEVE: We are away, Trev. This is the most isolated city on the planet. Can't get much more away than that.

TREV: Christ, it's hot tonight.

STEVE: Yeah. I can feel madness in the air. [*He sniffs at the air.*] I can smell it.

TREV: At one forty-five in the mornin'? Wouldn't be much madness left in the air. You got that look in your eye.

ANNOUNCEMENT: *[voice-over] Doors closing.*

STEVE *smiles at him and widens his eyes.*

STEVE: My ex moved into one of those new housing estates. [*Indicating out the window*] Just up there somewhere between the station and the river. Next to one of those fuckin' fake lakes. You know, those ones with the gushing fountains. Hate new housing estates.

TREV: Yeah?

STEVE: They got no smell. No one's ever fucked in them. Or died in them. They got no ghosts.

TREV: It's a safe place to bring up ya kids, mate.

STEVE: Exactly.

TREV: Every history's gotta start somewhere.

STEVE: Nah. History stops here. No one's makin' history anymore, Trev. Ya gotta have balls to do that.

TREV: So ya reckon we just spend the rest of our life… lookin' backwards?

STEVE: Not us.

TREV: Where do we look?

STEVE: Over our shoulder.

> *There is the deafening sound of screeching rubber from outside the train. Then the revving of a V8 engine that seems to last the entire length of a road. Both of them glance in its direction then back at each other.*

TREV: Who was that masked man?

STEVE: Dunno, but he left his scent behind.

TREV: Is he… the one?

STEVE: The prophet?

TREV: Nah.

STEVE: The Messiah?

TREV: Nah.

STEVE: A relative?

TREV: Could be. How do we know it's a he?

STEVE: It's a he. Were you impressed?

TREV: More than that, mate. I was… aroused. Strangely.

STEVE: Fair enough. You're only human.

ANNOUNCEMENT: [voice-over] Next station: Bassendean.

> TREV *starts singing the Rolf Harris song 'Big Dog' and playing an imaginary wobble board.*

STEVE: Shut up! Every time we go past Bassendean, ya start singin' a Rolf Harris song. Just tonight… don't. Gimme somethin' else.

TREV: [*mocking*] Oooo! I don't have anything else to give. Don't ya be knockin' Rolf, mate. He's a true original.

STEVE: I'm not knockin' Rolf, I'm knockin' you.

ANNOUNCEMENT: [voice-over] Doors closing.

> TREV *starts doing the Rolf Harris signature panting noise.*

STEVE: You'll hyper-ventilate, ya know. I passed out doin' that too much when I was a kid.

TREV: So you were a Rolf fan.

STEVE: I'll tell ya a story.

TREV: Love a story.

STEVE: Shut up. 1979. This whole fuckin' town is going ballistic 'cause it's our hundred-and-fiftieth anniversary. Down on Riverside Drive. They got this huge stage set up. It's the night of nights. Rolf Harris is the star attraction.

TREV: Who else?

STEVE: Shut up. So Rolf is whippin' the crowd up into a frenzy. He's got his wobble board out, and he's just done the twelve-inch version of *Two Little Fuckin' Boys*, when he invites the crowd to pant right along with him. Picture it. Ten thousand mums, dads and little kiddies all goin'… [*Panting*] Half the town passes out. Do you know how many brain cells were obliterated that night? This city has never recovered from it.

TREV: Where were you?

STEVE: I was coppin' a feel behind the chicko roll van. It's the only thing that saved me. [*Pause.*] Can we change the fuckin' subject?

TREV: You change the subject.

STEVE: Anythin' on the news this mornin'?

TREV: The news? What… Steve Leibmann and Tracy bloody Grimshaw?

STEVE: Well, that's the only news in the mornin'.

TREV: I never watch the morning news.

STEVE: Well, that's probably why ya totally ignorant as to what's goin' on outside ya lounge room.

TREV: What are ya talkin' about? Just 'cause I can't stand watchin' smiley Steve tell me about another disaster, man-made or natural, goin' on somewhere in the world, while he's holdin' a coffee in one hand and a croissant in the other. Mate, the only thing I'm interested in seein' on that programme is smiley Steve goin' down on his stinkin' hands and knees, look at us straight down the camera, and tell us to abandon all hope 'cause the world is fucked! Then I can get on with me day.

STEVE: That's a little heavy-handed, don't ya think?

TREV: I prefer the up-front approach.

ANNOUNCEMENT: [*voice-over*] *Next station: Bayswater.*

> *The doors slide open for the first time. A beautiful woman strides into the train. She looks very unsure about the situation but eventually seats herself opposite.*

ANNOUNCEMENT: [voice-over] Doors closing.

TREV: Sometimes… I just love this town.

STEVE: Perth's a beautiful place.

TREV: Beautiful place.

STEVE: Wouldn't live anywhere else.

TREV: Great people.

STEVE: Oh! Gotta love the locals. Always ready to have a laugh and a beer with ya while ya watchin' the sun sink into the ocean…

TREV: Or they'll bash and rape ya grandma. Not much in between. [*Pause.*] Fuck, it is so hot! Open a window.

STEVE: You can't open a window on a moving train, ya gork. That's why they have air conditioning.

TREV: Really? Stroke of genius that little slice of council plannin' was. The air conditioning is not workin'.

STEVE: Well, if you'd paid any taxes in the last five years you'd have something to complain about.

TREV: I'm gonna smash a window in here in a sec!

STEVE: Shut ya whingein'. You'll have a cold beer down ya gullet soon.

TREV: Yeah, well it's a long way to Freo.

> *Pause.*

STEVE: 'Scuse me, miss. I know you're gonna think this is terribly forward of me, but you are dead-set the most beautiful woman that I've ever seen catch this train before. Dead-set.

> *She says nothing but smiles awkwardly, not quite sure where to look.*

TREV: Tsk, tsk, you've made her all shy now.

> STEVE *sings the first couple of lines from the Hoodoo Gurus' song, 'Like Wow—Wipeout'.*

STEVE: Ya know I was in Prague once. Years ago. Woulda been ten years ago. And on their trains, this voice comes over the loudspeaker at every stop. Great big booming mother of a voice and I learnt this off by heart… it says: *'Ukonete Vystup A Nastup Dvere Se Zavyraji'.* Every fuckin' stop. And it sounds like the start of the revolution or somethin'. No bullshit. It sends chills up ya spine. And ya know what it means? 'Stand clear, doors closing.' I nearly pissed myself.

ANNOUNCEMENT: *[voice-over] Next station: Maylands.*

TREV: *[imitating]* 'Next station: Maylands.' Sounds like a silent fart to me. *[He lifts his arse cheek on Maylands to demonstrate.]* 'Next station: Maylands.'

STEVE: You are a seriously fucked-up individual. *[He turns to the woman.]* Please let me apologise for my mate here. He's only a kid. He's embarrassing but... he's got nowhere else to go. He tags along with me 'cause I make his life richer. It's better than havin' him wanderin' the streets by himself.

TREV: Jesus, you are smooth. She looks so impressed by your display of loyalty, mate.

ANNOUNCEMENT: *[voice-over] Doors closing.*

> *They stare at each other with dead eyes and knowing grins.*

STEVE: Face it, you're a dangerous man. You should be locked away.

TREV: Not this week.

> *He rolls his head around almost meditatively, then breathes in very slowly through his nose.*

It's a beautiful night.

STEVE: *[to* LISA*]* So, ah... do you have a name?

> *She glances at her watch.*

I can't help bein' nosey. I like to be a part of people's lives. It's just my nature. I'm up-front.

> *No response.*

You look like a... Simone or a... Beatrice.

> *She gives a half smile.*

TREV: Wo-ho. We have lift-off. I think ya got a grimace out of her. Give the man a kewpie doll.

STEVE: Shut up, ya thug. That is a beautiful smile. You could break a man's back with that smile.

LISA: My name's Lisa.

STEVE: Lissssa.

LISA: I have a grandmother called Beatrice.

STEVE: You're shittin' me? My dad's grandma was called Beatrice.

LISA: It's a very old-fashioned name.

STEVE: This is meant to be.

TREV: The Beatrice connection.

STEVE: Shut up! So where are ya off to… Lisa?

LISA: Fremantle.

STEVE: Goin' all the way.

LISA: That's right.

STEVE: So what ya been up to tonight?

LISA: Nothing too exciting. I went to the gym.

STEVE: The gym? So ya like to keep healthy, do ya?

LISA: Yes. But I'm not obsessive.

STEVE: So why would a glorious-lookin' woman such as yourself be travelling alone on the last train of the day? Could be very dangerous.

LISA: There's always at least five guards on every suburban train. Especially at two AM.

TREV: [*laughing*] She hasn't heard.

LISA: What?

STEVE: Guards are on strike tonight, darlin'. Look around. That's why there's no one else on the train. Like I said, could be very dangerous.

LISA: You tell me. Am I safe on this train?

He gives her what appears to be a reassuring smile.

ANNOUNCEMENT: [*voice-over*] *Next station: Claisebrook.*

TREV: [*standing up*] Claisebrook. Claisebrook. Who the fuck would live in Claisebrook?

He presses the button and yells out the open doors.

Get a life, Claisebrook!

STEVE: Siddown.

ANNOUNCEMENT: [*voice-over*] *Doors closing.*

TREV: [*mimicking*] 'Doors closing.' [*He pulls his crotch away from the closing doors at the last second.*] I reckon if you were from Claisebrook, gettin' ya dick caught in the doors would have to be the single most exciting event of ya dog's breath of a life. Do you wanna see the dying fish?

> *He falls to the floor and does his dying fish impersonation.* LISA *laughs.* STEVE *groans.*

She's laughin'. She loves me!

STEVE: She's laughin' at you, ya dickweed.

TREV: You're just jealous 'cause I'm doin' better than you.

STEVE: I apologise again, Lisa, but there truly is no honour amongst scumbags.

LISA: That's alright.

> *She takes out a book.*

STEVE: What are ya readin'?

LISA: Oh, it's just study material.

STEVE: So what are ya studying?

LISA: I'm a law student.

> TREV *laughs very loudly.*

What's so funny?

TREV: Oh, nothin'. It's just our favourite topic of conversation, that's all.

LISA: What's on your tattoo?

> *He looks at her for a little while before answering.*

STEVE: Red Sleeves.

LISA: Sorry?

STEVE: Red Sleeves. He's an Apache war chief. That's the Apache war sign on the outside. At the age of seventy, he could still outride and outfight anyone in his tribe. He defended his people against the Mexicans, the Spaniards and the white invaders. He was eventually betrayed by the white man like the rest of his people. They put two musket bullets into him then cut off his head and sold it to a museum. Greatest warriors that ever lived, the Apache. They'd die for their children, their women… And sometimes their horse.

ANNOUNCEMENT: *[voice-over] Next station: McIver.*

> *He stares up at the loudspeaker with contempt. His mood has darkened.*

STEVE: Hate this fuckin' town.

> *He gets up and walks down the carriage and stares out the window.*

TREV: So, Lisssa. Do ya have a boyfriend?

LISA: Why do you want to know?

TREV: Just bein' sociable. Hey, come away from those open doors, mate. You'll catch ya death.

ANNOUNCEMENT: *[voice-over] Doors closing.*

> *He turns his back to her.*

My mum used to say that to me all the time. Catch ya death.

> *He grabs at something in mid-air with one hand, then slowly brings his upturned closed fist down between them. He stares at her and says nothing, then opens his fist suddenly and yells.*

Bahhh!

STEVE: Get ya fuckin' legs off the seat. Can't ya read the signs?

> *He sits down next to* TREV.

So whadda ya reckon, Lisa? Is anybody else gonna get on this train or have we got it all to ourselves?

LISA: I'd say it's a fifty-fifty chance. It's a long way to Fremantle.

STEVE: That's right, it is a long way to Freo. I reckon you'll get off at Perth station.

LISA: Really? Very expensive to get a cab from here to Fremantle. I'm only a student, remember.

TREV: *[holding out his hand to his mate]* Twenty bucks she gets off in Perth.

> *He doesn't react for a while, just keeps staring at her. Then he slowly goes to take his hand. He pulls back at the last second.*

STEVE: She stays and more people will join the train. Double or nothing.

TREV: Ya gotta be shittin' me. This train would be deserted if the guards *weren't* on strike. Perth's a dangerous place, mate, haven't ya heard? *[He holds out his hand.]* Shake, K'mosobi.

> *The two men sit opposite her and just stare at her. She does the same back. They are moving in a gentle motion with the train.*

ANNOUNCEMENT: *[voice-over] Next station: Perth.*

TREV: Now see… I don't have any problems with the way she says that. It's like ya know ya comin' into the big one. *[Imitating]* 'Next station:

Perth.' It's like… here's the one you've all been waitin' for, folks…
Perth. It's very confident and detailed work.

> *Silence.* TREV *starts singing 'Jackson' (Nancy Sinatra/Lee Hazle-wood) very gently. The words sort of crawl out of his mouth.*

> *The sound of the train pulling into a station. Lights up on the platform. The train has stopped at Perth Central. Two more people sit opposite them: a man in black, about mid-thirties [the* WRITER*], and a woman in her forties [*MAUREEN*], wearing tracksuit pants and carrying some bags.*

> STEVE *smiles and holds out his hand to receive twenty dollars from a reluctant* TREV. LISA *hasn't moved. Everyone is avoiding each other's gaze except for the thugs who are assessing the situation. The* MAN *in the black coat takes out what looks like a diary and begins writing something.*

ANNOUNCEMENT: *[voice-over] This train goes to Fremantle stopping all stations. Doors closing.*

STEVE: *[gleefully pocketing the money]* Ukonete Vystup A Nastup Dvere Se Zavyraji!

TREV: Double or nothing we take on more passengers before Freo.

STEVE: Bash it up your ass. We got enough for a party right here. So when's the last time anyone ever told you how beautiful you are, Lisa?

LISA: You did about ten minutes ago.

STEVE: Shame, isn't it?

LISA: What is?

STEVE: How blokes can't speak their mind anymore. How a man can't just walk up to a woman on the street and tell her that he's glad he got out of bed this morning just so's he got to gaze upon her radiant features. Naa. Ya can't do that anymore. They tell you to fuck off or they think ya want somethin' from them. You don't think I want somethin' from you, do ya Lisa?

LISA: I think you've got what you wanted. I stayed on the train.

STEVE: Yes, you did. Yes, you did. And ya don't look so scared anymore.

TREV: Double or nothing she gets off before Freo.

STEVE: Shut up, I'm talking to Lisa.

> *He sits down next to* LISA.

Truth is… I do want something from you.

LISA: Really?

STEVE: Look… the thing you need to know about me is that I love women, love 'em. I… love kids… I… love animals… most animals. I… wanna get your number. Let's go out to dinner. I haven't been to a restaurant in five years. Do ya wanna go for a walk along the beach at sunset? Don't laugh at me, I'm serious.

ANNOUNCEMENT: [voice-over] Next station: City West.

LISA: You don't even know me.

STEVE: Does anyone know anyone?

LISA: You're crazy.

TREV: I bet you know lots of shakers and movers, Lisa.

LISA: Sorry, I'm not sure what you mean.

TREV: You know. People who like movin' and shakin', shakin' and movin'. You know, people who think it's so fuckin' important that we fill every second of our life with a purpose.

ANNOUNCEMENT: [voice-over] Doors closing.

TREV: Ya know, I was picked up for loitering the other day. For doin' nothin'. Like it's a crime. I was just hangin' out on the street corner mindin' my own business and a cop pulls over on his bike. He thought he was from *Chips*. Cop says to me, 'What are you doin' here, mate?' I says, 'Same as you, officer. Waitin' to die.' So he arrests me. [*Pause.*] How can you get arrested for doin' nothin', when there's nothin' to do.

LISA: He might've mistaken you for a car thief or something.

TREV: Really. Jeez, I never thought I looked like a car thief. I mean… he asked for my driver's license and I didn't have one, so maybe that got him thinkin'. I know I don't look like a shaker and a mover.

STEVE: Poor Trev. He's been hangin' around me ever since I stopped him from hangin' himself. He'd been slashin' up over all sorts of stuff. Family stuff mainly. The screws get no training in how to resuscitate a dyin' prisoner. Thank fuck I knew how to. You know they spend more money on prisons than they do on universities and none of the screws have any first-aid trainin'.

TREV: Fifty-five grand a year on each prisoner it costs the state. Why don't they just give that to me when I get out!

STEVE: It's about punishment, not rehabilitation. You know that, Trev. The more scumbags like us they lock away, the safer the middle class feel in their beds at night.

TREV: God bless 'em.

STEVE: The middle class get to see shrinks and have Prozac prescribed and we get thrown in the clink for our choice of... narcotic. We're all just tryin' to dull our pain, aren't we?

> *Over the loudspeakers, classical music is pumping out.* STEVE *starts humming along.*

That's just beautiful, isn't it? So tell me, Lisa, as a good tax-paying citizen, do ya reckon this music is soothing the savage beast on our public transport system?

LISA: I'm not sure. I mean... I find it quite annoying. I'm not big on classical music myself. It makes me feel like I'm in an elevator.

STEVE: What's it doin' for you, Trev?

TREV: [*widening his eyes and staring ahead glassily*] Dunno, I'm comin' over all queer. I feel calmer for some reason.

STEVE: Yeah, same here.

TREV: Yeah, I was lookin' forward to some grievous bodily harm tonight but now I just wanna waltz.

STEVE: [*holding his hand out to her*] Would you like to dance, Lisa?

LISA: You are unbelievable.

> *She looks away with a half smile. He keeps his hand held out to her for ten seconds, totally immobile, then swiftly whips it away.*

STEVE: You don't believe I can dance, do ya?

LISA: No, it's not that, it's just...

STEVE: 'Cause I can you know.

> *Pause.*

LISA: So where did you learn?

STEVE: Prison.

LISA: Right. [*Pause.*] What sort of dancing?

STEVE: Ballroom, a bit of Latin. Cha-cha-cha.

LISA: Who was your dance partner?

STEVE: Blokes used to dance with blokes. No big deal.

LISA: Well, you're one up on me then.

STEVE: Why? 'Cause ya never been to prison?

LISA: [*laughing*] No, because I can't dance.

STEVE: Then let me show you.

LISA: Sorry. No. Thank you anyway.

ANNOUNCEMENT: [voice-over] Next station: Subiaco.

STEVE: So where do you live, Lisa?

LISA: You don't need to know that.

STEVE: You're bein' very cagey, Lisa. I'm hardly gonna find out your address just because ya tell me what suburb you're from. I don't even know ya last name.

LISA: I just don't give out information to people I don't know on public transport.

ANNOUNCEMENT: [voice-over] Doors closing.

STEVE: Fair enough. Don't ya trust people, Lisa?

TREV: She doesn't trust you, mate.

LISA: I don't actually. Most people I meet either want to sell you something or fuck you.

STEVE: [*laughing*] That's beautiful! I'll pay that one.

TREV: She's got you sussed.

STEVE: Ya gonna make a beautiful lawyer. Ask me about myself.

LISA: Why?

STEVE: Ah… no reason. Just love opening up to people.

> *Pause.*

LISA: Whereabouts are you from?

STEVE: From? From… from… Stupid word that. I've lived in Beechboro all my life.

LISA: Right. Why are you going to Fremantle?

STEVE: 'Cause the train doesn't go any further.

LISA: When did you get out of prison?

STEVE: Just last week in fact.

LISA: How long were you in for?

STEVE: This time… only six months.

LISA: How many times have you been in?

STEVE: That was my fourth.

LISA: How did you handle being inside?

STEVE: Well, it's all a state of mind really. When I was a kid I used to think that if I couldn't see something, it didn't exist. When I turned my back on something, it just disappeared. That's what I did when I went into the joint. I pretended that it didn't matter what was happening in the outside world because it didn't exist anymore. It's a very… Genet experience.

LISA: Is it as bad as they say? I mean, aren't they trying to improve conditions by privatising some of them?

TREV: It's not fuckin' Woollies, love.

Pause.

LISA: Um… what's your name?

STEVE: Don't you wanna know why I was in there?

LISA: That's your business. It's not—

STEVE: I slit a guy from rib to waist. Outside a nightclub. Then I started kickin' his head in.

LISA: That's nice. Why did you do that?

STEVE: 'Cause he put a knife through me leg.

LISA: What for?

STEVE: Ya don't need a reason where I'm from, but it just so happens he was hassling my girlfriend. So I told him to fuck off. He was full of piss and he was young, so he wanted to fight me. I told him to come back when his balls had dropped. Then he pulled a knife on me.

ANNOUNCEMENT: *[voice-over] Next station: Daglish.*

LISA: Did he die?

STEVE: Ya think I woulda been out in six months if he had? You're studying law, you should know that.

LISA: Corporate law. So… is this guy all right now?

STEVE: Nnnno… not really. I remember there bein' blood all over the walls and him screaming out, 'You're killin' me, stop it!' So I did.

LISA: I don't think I wanna ask you any more questions, okay?

STEVE: That's a shame. I'm a complex and multi-faceted individual,

Lisa. It's a pity you don't want to inquire beyond my criminal exploits.

She says nothing.

Am I scaring you, Lisa?

ANNOUNCEMENT: *[voice-over] Doors closing.*

TREV: Scezinski.

STEVE: Eh?

TREV: Scezinski. That's her last name. It's written on one of her study books. Can't be too many Scezinskis that live around here.

LISA: [*standing up hurriedly*] Fuck off! Just fuck off, okay!

> STEVE *walks over to* TREV, *then pushes his head into the pole.*

STEVE: Hey. Hey! Don't be a prick, okay?!

> *He releases him.*

You can sit down, Lisa, it's all right. Don't worry about him. He doesn't have a life.

> *Pause.* LISA *doesn't move.*

Now I know who you remind me of. My grandma as a young woman. I mean she was absolutely beautiful. Ava Gardner, I'm not kidding. Her son was a waste of space. So was his wife. But she was noble, proud, beautiful. I know nothin' about my family before her. It's like we just crawled up outta the gutter and began. Whadda ya reckon they're gonna think when they look back at photos of us in the future? That we were a noble proud people? I mean… most of the photos of Trev, he's off his face and I look like I wanna kill someone…

MAUREEN: Stop it!

> *The woman in the tracksuit pants who has been looking down at the ground with her arms folded has spoken up for the first time.*

You've had your fun, now leave her alone.

TREV: And you are?

MAUREEN: Look, she just wants to go to Freo. So why don't you stop giving her a hard time.

STEVE: Excuse me, lady, but we're just passin' the time here.

MAUREEN: Yes, by scaring the bloody life out of this poor girl. You know…

a person should be able to catch a train from one suburb to another without having to fear for their safety.

TREV: Well, see the thing is… ah… what's ya name?

MAUREEN: It's Maureen.

TREV: Maureen… is that prior to you getting' on the train in Perth, we'd… ah… already established a… relationship here with Miss Lisa. You know… we'd made a connection.

MAUREEN: Well, I'm not sure that's what she'd call it. It's a bloody disgrace what's happening in this town. There's no respect anymore for anyone. You know… just because there are no guards on tonight, doesn't give you the right to harass innocent people who are going about their business.

STEVE: Did you feel harassed, Lisa?

LISA *sits down and says nothing.*

MAUREEN: This sort of shit goes on every night on these trains and no one ever does anything about it. No one ever steps in to help. It's like that footage they kept playing on the news over and over again, of that poor bastard getting the bejesus kicked out of him on the train. Everyone just walked past it. Right on past it. He was probably one of your mates. Well, I've had enough of it.

TREV: Ya shouldn't watch the news, Maureen. It fucks with ya head.

MAUREEN: This town has turned into a bloody sewer populated by sewer rats.

STEVE *starts clapping.*

STEVE: Good for you, Maureen. You've shown a lotta courage tonight. I respect courage.

MAUREEN: Don't you take the piss outta me, you mongrel!

STEVE: I'm not takin' the piss outta ya. You're a woman of principle.

MAUREEN: [*reaching into her pocket and giving* LISA *twenty dollars*] Take this, love. Get off at Karrakatta and get yourself a cab to Freo. You'll be safer out there than you are in here. I'll make sure they don't follow you. [*Into her mobile*] Yes, I'd like a cab for Karrakatta station, thank you… For a Lisa… What address are you going to, love? [*Looking at the two thugs*] Um… she'll tell you when you pick her up. Can you please be quick because she's going to be standing out there all by herself... Ta. [*She hangs up.*] Shouldn't be too long.

ANNOUNCEMENT: *[voice-over] Next station: Karrakatta.*

> *The train stops.* LISA *doesn't move.* MAUREEN *gets up and opens the doors.*

MAUREEN: Come on, love! Go! What are you doing? Get out of the train! You've gotta get out of this train now!

ANNOUNCEMENT: *[voice-over] Doors closing.*

MAUREEN: Oh, for fuck's sake!

> MAUREEN *sits down heavily.*

TREV: Me mum's buried there. So's me grandpop. And me best mate Tony. He topped himself last year. I hate the place.

LISA: I never get off at Karrakatta.

> *She hands* MAUREEN *the money back.*

Thanks.

STEVE: We like you, Maureen. Where ya from?

From left: Andrea Moor as Maureen, Rebecca Massey as Lisa and Brett Stiller as Trev in the 2001 Griffin Theatre production in Sydney. (Photo: Robert McFarlane)

MAUREEN *says nothing.*

Look… we're goin' all the way through to Freo. All of us. 'Course I can't speak for the gentleman here who's been scribblin' away like a madman ever since he got on.

The WRITER *doesn't even look up.*

Right. So we'll behave, okay? Won't hurt to make a bit a small talk. Will it? Maybe we could make some big talk. A bit starved for big talk from people these days. No one seems to have the time.

MAUREEN: Maybe people are just choosy about who they talk to.

STEVE: Shame, isn't it?

MAUREEN: What is?

STEVE: All the lack of trust that's floatin' around out there.

MAUREEN: Yeah, well it's men like yourself that've caused that, haven't you?

TREV: That's a bit harsh.

STEVE: And what sort of men are we, Maureen?

MAUREEN: The sort of men that keep people home at night behind locked doors.

STEVE: Is that right?

MAUREEN: That's right. A friend of mine was bashed at an ATM last week. He was just getting some money out to pay for his daughter's school books! It's disgusting. If that was that mugger's contribution to society… then better that they were never born.

STEVE: Well, that mugger has got a story to tell as well.

MAUREEN: I'm sorry, I'm not interested in hearing it.

STEVE: Then on and on it goes. Thing is… you wouldn't know to look at us, but… ah… Trev and I are pretty smart dudes. True, we've been in and outta Casuarina a few times, but we used our time wisely. We educated ourselves, did a lot of courses. Read a lot of books. We're definitely wiser men for havin' been in the joint.

TREV: Speak for yourself! I wasn't a drug addict before I went inside.

STEVE: You'd never met a blackfella before either, had ya?

TREV: Prison's a revolving door.

MAUREEN: I bet you learnt to have a lotta respect for women in that place as well.

STEVE: [*sighing heavily*] Lisa, I'd like to apologise to you on behalf of Trev and myself. If we caused you any grief, I am truly sorry. Say sorry, Trev.

> *He just lays there.*

Say fuckin' sorry!

TREV: [*mumbling*] Sorry.

LISA: It's okay.

STEVE: I won't, however, back down on my opinion that you are a glorious-looking woman. But I will keep it to myself from now on.

MAUREEN: See. Do you have to…?

LISA: Look, it's fine. Really. I can look after myself. They were actually quite… amusing before we got to Perth. I get the train all the time and… I attract attention all the time as well. I'm used to it. It used to annoy the hell out of me, but it's easier to catch the train to Freo than it is to drive. So I just ignore it mostly. To tell the truth, I'd rather put up with them than some of the sleazy businessmen that try and chat me up. At least these guys are honest. Although he's a bit weird.

> *She gestures towards* TREV.

TREV: You'll catch ya death…

STEVE: So everything is sweet, mmm? Where did you say you were from, Maureen?

MAUREEN: I didn't.

STEVE: Come on, we're all friends here now, aren't we?

MAUREEN: Hardly.

ANNOUNCEMENT: [*voice-over*] Next station: Shenton Park.

MAUREEN: I'm originally from London. Actually. But now I live in Girrawheen.

STEVE: Bullshit! That's where Trev lives. Don't ya, Trev?

TREV: You poor bitch. Bunghole of the earth. I shoulda put a match to it years ago.

ANNOUNCEMENT: [*voice-over*] Doors closing.

> MAUREEN *looks at him after this comment and manages a wry smile. She says nothing at first then breaks out into a quiet chuckle, shaking her head.* STEVE *pulls out an unopened bottle*

of Jack Daniels.

STEVE: Have a drink, Maureen.

He passes her the bottle and pours himself a capful. She hesitates, then accepts it.

[*Holding the cap up in front of him*] To Girrawheen. [*He sculls it.*] Drink it, Maureen. Ya might die in a tragic gardening accident tomorrow.

She drinks it down in great big gulps like she needs it.

Whoa there. Leave some for Trev.

TREV: [*yodelling like an old cowboy*] 'I left my heart in Girrawheen. It took my liver and my spleeeen.'

STEVE: Drink, Lisa?

LISA: No thanks.

STEVE: You know, Lisa, there's more to you than meets the eye.

LISA: Really?

STEVE: Really. There's a reason why you didn't get off this train in Perth.

LISA: I told you. It's an expensive cab ride.

STEVE: Na, it's something else. Can't quite work it out. [*Clapping his hands together*] Anyway, not ta worry. We're all together now. That's a bloody big suitcase ya dragging to Freo, Maureen. Are ya movin' there?

MAUREEN: You really are a nosey bastard, aren't you? Actually you're quite good-lookin'. For a thug.

STEVE: Says the girl from Girrawheen.

He snatches the bottle from her.

Be nice or you won't get any more.

He refills his cap, then gives it back to her. She has another huge swig.

There's something troubling you, isn't there? And it's not just us.

MAUREEN: It could be the heat. There's somethin' weird in the air tonight. [*Pause.*] I've left my husband.

LISA: You'd be enjoying that drink then.

STEVE: Is he causin' ya some grief?

MAUREEN: None of your friggin' business.

STEVE: I know, Maureen, but, ah… it might help to talk about it.

MAUREEN: You are unbelievable. A minute ago I was about to call the cops on you and now you want me to spill my guts out to you.

STEVE: There's a free bourbon in it.

She stares at him then takes the bourbon.

MAUREEN: Well… you see… we didn't start off too well 'cause the day he asks me to marry him, he took me to the spot where his mother had died. She choked to death in a restaurant. So we're sitting in this family restaurant in Morley… and he asks me for my hand in marriage… and I was thinking how bloody sad and weird this was, but I felt really sorry for him and he was quite handsome and captain of the local darts team, so I said yes. That was the fourth of May 1979. And now… well… it's just… you know, he drinks. [*She takes another huge swig from the bottle.*] Mostly after the footy and he drives home. I tell him he's gonna get caught one day but he just tells me to mind my own business. And he comes in so shitty 'cause his footy team loses every week. Every single week. And he always kicks the cat. And I say, 'Don't take it out on that poor defenceless creature. It's not her fault your team is so useless. I mean, have a look at your forward line. There's the problem. There's the bloody problem.' And he never tells me what's going on inside his head. Ever. All his friends are useless bloody drunks with no manners. I can't stand them. I've tried to get him interested in other things but he's just too lazy and… stupid. And then he tells me that I never get off my fat ass and go out and do anything different myself and, well… he's right, but at least I think about doing something else. I mean… some of my friends are very interesting. Lara, she's my best friend… she's learning how to read tarot cards, and Jean, she's got a hair loss problem and… she's had to seek out herbal remedies from exotic parts of the world. And… [*starting to cry*] I just want him to get out of the house, that's all. Just… leave me alone for a while. So that I can… think… about… something else. I don't know what. I wish he'd just go away. Just so that… I can listen to my heart for a while.

ANNOUNCEMENT: [*voice-over*] *Next station: Loch Street.*

STEVE: Feel better?

MAUREEN: No, I frigging don't!

STEVE: Maureen, for no cost at all, I am about to offer to make your life better. Give me your address, you stay and have a drink with Trev here, and I'll nip around to your place and your husband will be no more. Easy as that. Think about it.

ANNOUNCEMENT: *[voice-over] Doors closing.*

There is no reply for a while.

MAUREEN: No. He's all right… I guess.

STEVE: You're not convincing anyone, Maureen. I know his type because I used to be one of 'em.

MAUREEN: And now you're not?

STEVE: Naah. I'm worse. Look, you'll be better off without him.

MAUREEN: Ya can't just kill him!

STEVE: He's a prick, Maureen. I know. Do ya wish he was better, faster, stronger? Well, guess what, darlin', so does he. Make no mistake about it, men are fucked. We're hideous creatures. And it's a real shame, ya know, 'cause last time I woke up I was one. But I'll make him kiss the ground upon which you walk or rue the day he ever crawled into your life.

MAUREEN: Why am I talking to a psycho for?

TREV: Psycho… psychiatrist. Not much difference there.

STEVE: Shut up. Do ya have kids, Maureen?

MAUREEN: I got three.

STEVE: Hang onto your kids. But when the time is right, help them run as far away as possible. Before the rot sets in.

MAUREEN: They've all moved outta home. [*Pause.*] I'm a good mother.

LISA: He's just joking, Maureen. He won't hurt your husband.

STEVE: Well… only on Maureen's request.

TREV: Why don't ya go to Rotto, Maureen, and do a Shirley Valentine. I'm sure you'll meet a nice crayfisherman over there.

MAUREEN *bursts out half laughing, half crying.*

LISA: Why don't you kick him out of the house?

MAUREEN: Ever tried to move a dead man?

ANNOUNCEMENT: [voice-over] Next station: Showgrounds.

LISA: I used to go to the Royal Show every year when I was a kid. I haven't been for… ten years.

STEVE: I used to jump the fence every year. Never paid to get in. There was a hole in the fence at—

LISA: Ten Judge Avenue. That's famous, that hole. It used to be right behind the bouncing castle.

STEVE: [*laughing*] You know it! Musta been closed up for years now.

ANNOUNCEMENT: [voice-over] Doors closing.

TREV: I saw a guy choke on his own spew on the Wild West Roundup.

LISA: Isn't that an urban myth?

TREV: Callin' me a liar?

> TREV *snatches the bottle back from* MAUREEN.

Don't drink all the JD, thank you. [*Taking a swig*] Me and my mate Fred used ta hide in the haunted horror house and feel up every chick that went through. They didn't think anything was wrong, 'cause that's what happens when ya go in the haunted horror house. People touch ya up to scare ya. [*Imitating a showground voice*] 'Come to the haunted horror house! Come to the haunted horror house!'

LISA: That's gross!

TREV: Not really. We were just part of the whole haunted horror house experience.

LISA: I used to go in there all the time.

STEVE: Don't ya feel stupid lookin' back on that, Trev?

TREV: Nah, we had a ball. Better fun than walkin' around lookin' at chickens and goats.

> *Pause.*

STEVE: Ya gotta forgive him. He's from bad stock. His old man's got this knack of being present at some of Perth's most forgettable moments.

TREV: Piss off. What about the first State of Origin match in '77? He took me there to see to see the big V go down. Seven goals to one in the first quarter. Barry Cable, what a champion.

STEVE: Yeah, you were there. Ya woulda been all of two years old. Your old man started an all-in brawl before the first bounce. He nearly threw a guy to his death from the top level of the grandstand.

TREV: Yeah, some prick from Ballarat called Gary Sidebottom a poofter! Then he got stuck into Archie Duda.

STEVE: Archie Duda wasn't even playin', mate!

TREV: Doesn't matter. He's a fuckin' Sandgroper, isn't he?

STEVE: He was a fuckin' East Perth player! Where was his head at? If he'd—

MAUREEN: Can… we not talk about the footy… please?! I feel like I haven't left the house. [*Pause.*] I wish I hadn't opened up to you people. I feel ridiculous.

ANNOUNCEMENT: *[voice-over] Next station: Claremont.*

MAUREEN: I might get off here. This was a stupid idea.

> *She goes over to the doors and stares out into the blackness. She sits down heavily on her suitcase.*

ANNOUNCEMENT: *[voice-over] Doors closing.*

LISA: Why don't you stay with one of your children?

MAUREEN: I… don't want to be a burden.

TREV: That's what my mum used ta say. I don't wanna be a burden. Then one day she just dropped dead. Left me wishin' I'd let her be a burden. Just once.

> *No one speaks for a while.*

STEVE: [*standing up*] Well, haven't we got one happy little train chuffin' along here?! Ya gotta sing. It's the only way. Sometimes ya just gotta close your eyes and just sing it out!

TREV: Golly, gee, whizzo. Thank you, Judith Durham.

> *He sings some of 'Morningtown Ride' (The Seekers).*

STEVE: I'm serious. [*Pointing to his tattoo*] Red Sleeves once said: 'I sing for my people and for no other reason'. I thought that was amazing. I thought how fuckin' wild to have a people. Who are my people? Do I have a people? Is it, Trev? Most of my people can't stand each other's guts. They can't stand themselves. Ya gotta have a people. Anyway, doesn't matter. I can't sing.

TREV: You're from a people.

STEVE: Where?

TREV: Beechboro.

STEVE: That's a fuckin' suburb, it's not a people.

TREV: Who do ya think lives in the suburb? People. Your people are the Beechboro people.

He goes up to TREV, *puts his hands around his neck and lifts him above his head.*

STEVE: They… are… not… my… fuckin'… people!

They stay in that position like some absurd Mexican stand-off until TREV *starts gently singing some more of 'Morningtown Ride', in a strangled voice.*

STEVE *releases him and starts doing some bizarre tribal dance around the carriage to his singing. It is a very surreal image. During the course of the dance he has edged right up to the* WRITER *who has been writing the whole time and not acknowledging the action at all.* STEVE *very deftly snatches the man's notebook away from him.*

STEVE: What the fuck have you been doing in this little book… mate?

LISA: Stop it! He's not annoying anyone.

STEVE: No, but he's startin' to make me feel very uncomfortable.

LISA: Give it back to him.

TREV: [*to the* WRITER] I think she likes you, mate. Chicks always go for the dark mysterious types who sit in the corner and say fuck-all.

STEVE: That's 'cause most of 'em have got fuck-all to say. What ya writin' about, mate?

WRITER: Just doodling.

STEVE: Doooodling? Right. Mind if I have a look at your little doodles?

WRITER: Ah… I do actually.

He tries to snatch the notebook back. STEVE *grabs his wrist hard and holds it there.*

LISA: Leave him alone!

WRITER: It's personal.

STEVE lets go of his wrist.*

STEVE: You've been very unsociable, mate. Ya didn't even join in to our little open forum on Maureen's problem here.

WRITER: I like keeping to myself.

STEVE: And ya didn't step in when young Lisa here was obviously getting... distressed.

WRITER: Look, I just...

STEVE: Maureen did. She showed no fear.

WRITER: I'm sorry that I ignored you. Does that make you nervous?

STEVE: Something in this has kept you very occupied. But... it's none of my business so I'll give it back to you.

He goes to give the notebook back then hesitates.

No, I don't think I will.

He tosses it over to TREV.

If it's boring, you can have it back. What's in it, Trev?

TREV: [*opening it up and reading it aloud*] 'Red Sleeves sings for his people. Who are my people?' [*He flicks back a few pages.*] 'Are you a shaker and a mover, Lisa?' Hey, I said that. He's been writin' down everything we been sayin'. What... are you in the CIB or somethin', mate?

WRITER: Look, I'm... I was just bored. I jot down snippets of conversations sometimes. There's nothing in it. Can... I have my... notebook back... please?

TREV: Pretty bloody detailed snippets ya got here, mate. You're a regular stenographer.

MAUREEN: Will you just give it back to him?

TREV: You feature very strongly here too, Maureen.

MAUREEN: What? Why are you interested in what I've got to say?

TREV: Maybe ya husband hired him to keep a record of ya movements.

MAUREEN: Oh, please!

STEVE: Well, for someone who likes keepin' to himself, you seem to have taken an intense interest in what other people have been sayin'.

TREV: [*flicking back further through the book*] Listen to this. 'The tall thug stands up and does a bizarre Indian-like dance...'

STEVE: So who's the tall thug? You wouldn't be referring to me, would ya?

WRITER: Well... you guys call yourself thugs. I just... picked up on that.

STEVE: That's right, we do. It's a term of endearment between me and Trev. Doesn't give you the right to get that… familiar.

WRITER: Okay, I apologise. Give me my book back and I'll get off at the next stop.

STEVE: Nah, I don't think so. Don't know if I like bein' one of your little snippets. We might keep your book.

WRITER: All right.

ANNOUNCEMENT: *[voice-over] Next station: Swanbourne.*

> *The* WRITER *goes to get up.* STEVE *slams his arm around his throat, pinning him to the seat.*

STEVE: Tell me the fucking truth, mate!

LISA: Let him go!

WRITER: [*choking*] It's a play!

STEVE: What?

WRITER: I'm writing a play!

STEVE: A play?

WRITER: I'm just doing some research.

STEVE: Research? What's your play about?

WRITER: It's about people from… a similar background such as yourself.

STEVE: [*laughing*] Well, why didn't ya say so?

> *He releases him.*

ANNOUNCEMENT: *[voice-over] Doors closing.*

WRITER: I didn't think you'd like it very much.

TREV: Well, you'd be right there.

STEVE: So you're a… playwright?

WRITER: Well, I'm a writer. I just happen to be working on a play at the moment.

STEVE: Is that right? I woulda put my money on you bein' a faggot. He's not a faggot, Trev, he's a writer.

TREV: We had this bunch of actors come to Casuarina once. They put a play on. Did *Hamlet* for us.

WRITER: Did you like it?

TREV: Thought it was brilliant. We had three blokes try and hang themselves in their cell after the show.

*Tim Michin (left) as the writer and Grant Bowler as Steve in the 2002
Perth Theatre Company production. (Photo: Jon Green)*

WRITER: Well, it's pretty powerful stuff.

STEVE: So me and Trev are gonna be in your play? What about Lisa and Maureen here?

WRITER: No… look… it's not actually about you. It's about people… like you.

STEVE: What, like ex-cons?

WRITER: Sort of. They're from… a lower socio-economic background and they're potentially dangerous.

TREV: You mean a couple of losers?

WRITER: No. I don't see them as losers.

STEVE: So you catch a late-night train in the hope that there'll be a couple of scumbags on it just so's you can get some stuff for ya play.

WRITER: Well, I've got to get it from somewhere.

STEVE: How'd ya know we'd even be on this train?

WRITER: Because you always are. Or someone like you.

TREV: So we're the bad guys in the play.

WRITER: Look… I don't know. I haven't even got a story.

TREV: Well, I think you better work it out, mate. I think you better let us help you find a story.

STEVE: How about, 'Man in black coat gets thrown from moving train'?

ANNOUNCEMENT: *[voice-over] Next station: Grant Street.*

LISA: I think we should go.

STEVE: I think it would be in your best interest to put Trev in your play.

WRITER: I don't think that would work.

STEVE: Why not?

WRITER: Well, there's probably a character in here based on Trev, so… he might be a bit close to it to… perform it.

ANNOUNCEMENT: *[voice-over] Doors closing.*

TREV: Whadda ya mean?

WRITER: Well, you can't play you. Someone else has to play you.

TREV: Well, what's the fuckin' point in that? I play me all the time. Someone famous?

WRITER: Sorry?

TREV: Is someone famous gonna play me?

WRITER: Possibly.

TREV: I don't want it to be a play. Make it into a movie.

STEVE: So how does it feel to mix with the other side, mate? Are we dangerous enough for ya?

WRITER: I'm not interested in the fact that you're dangerous. I'm interested in why you're dangerous.

STEVE: Is that right? So if I cracked your fuckin' head open and sent you to the floor like a sack of turds, you're only gonna give a flying frog's fat ass about *why* I perpetrated a random act of violence against an upstanding member of our society.

WRITER: Yes.

STEVE: Bullshit. You'd do exactly what I'd do. You'd hunt me down or get some other fuckwit to do the job and squash me like a worm. And I'd deserve it. Are ya scared of me?

WRITER: No.

STEVE: Well, ya better hope I make your life a misery. Real soon. Otherwise there's no point in writin' about me is there?

WRITER: Um… look… I can see now that this is not such a good idea.

STEVE: No, no, no… ya can't turn back now. I'm startin' to see you as the voice of a very misunderstood section of our society. But you know… there's a million of me gettin' around, mate. And they'll all tell ya they had a tough life. You know, beaten up by their dad, in trouble with the cops, pisshead mum, rough school. A million fuckin' excuses why they turned out to be bad eggs. And I got all of the above… Oh yeah! Truth is, most of 'em are just bored. They leave their shit-ass state school and live on the dole in their diddly bum-fuck nowhere suburb. Before ya know it, ya got some girl up the duff and no money. She spends the day with a screamin' sprog and a fag in her mouth plonked in front of a daytime soap wearin' her tracky daks all day, dreamin' of bein' swept away by some Fabio and she just gets… fatter. But… her Centrelink payments have gone up and all her fat friends are waitin' in line behind her! It's a career move for 'em. Gettin' up the duff. And you… drink with ya mates, watch the footy and the highlight of the week is the local tavern has a skimpy barmaid every Friday. And ya know the rest of the world is havin' a better time. Ya just know it. The magazines are tellin' ya that, the newspapers, the telly. Everybody's richer, everybody's more beautiful, and everybody's got more... purpose. And ya thinkin', how do I make sense of this dog-ass life? And then one day ya just get hold of a gun. Ya don't even know what ya gonna do with it. It's like the sound of a V8 in the distance. It takes ya... somewhere else. [*Pause.*] I didn't see ya writin' any of this down. I'm spillin' my guts out in the name of art and you don't give a shit. What sort of writer are ya?

ANNOUNCEMENT: *[voice-over] Next station: Cottesloe.*

LISA: [*to the* WRITER] I think we should get off this stop.

WRITER: You go. I've got to stay.

LISA: No. It's gone too far.

STEVE: Do you two know each other?

WRITER: No. I think she's just looking out for my best interests.

LISA: C'mon, let's go.

WRITER: No.

LISA: Yes!

WRITER: You go.

LISA: Please! Let's... go!

STEVE: Nobody's goin' anywhere. You two do know each other.

LISA: Yes.

STEVE: Excuse me? Somebody's playin' silly buggers at our expense here.

ANNOUNCEMENT: *[voice-over] Doors closing.*

> LISA *goes over and presses the doors open.* TREV *goes over and blocks the doorway.*

TREV: [*shaking his head*] Uh, uh. You'll catch ya death.

ANNOUNCEMENT: *[voice-over] Doors closing.*

MAUREEN: Let her out!

STEVE: Shut up, Maureen! Not until I find out what the fuck is going on. Siddown, Lisa.

> *She doesn't move.*

Fucking *sit down*!

She sits down next to the WRITER *and takes his hand.*

So… are you two… friends?

LISA: We're seeing each other.

STEVE: The plot thickens. [*To the* WRITER] First of all… explain to me why you two pretended not to know each other and why your… fiancée here… has been flirting with us since she got on at Bayswater.

LISA: I wasn't flirting with you.

TREV: Ya weren't exactly runnin' away screaming. Everyone else does.

WRITER: Look… leave her alone. This is my idea.

STEVE: Do tell.

WRITER: Lisa wanted to help with my research, so I had this idea for her to… get on the train before me and get you two… talking to her… so that by the time I got on the situation was… you know, warmed up.

TREV: What do ya mean, warmed up?

WRITER: Well, I knew that you'd flirt with her because she's beautiful and that's the sort of… situation I wanted to witness.

STEVE: Why?

WRITER: I wanted to see you at your worst.

Pause.

STEVE: How do you feel about this, Trev?

TREV: Quite frankly, I feel used.

STEVE: Let me tell you something. This is not us at our worst. How did you know Trev and I were gonna be on this train?

He says nothing.

TREV: He's followed us before.

STEVE: What sort of gutless turd are you? Lettin' your girlfriend do your dirty work for ya. How do ya know somethin' wasn't gonna happen to her, eh? Ya know what the Apaches used to do to warriors that didn't protect their squaws?

LISA: Please, we're sorry.

STEVE: [*to* LISA] Don't you say another fucking word!

TREV: Well, I am fucking gobsmacked! Whadda ya reckon, Maureen? There's not a hero left in this town.

MAUREEN *has been quiet, sensing that the situation might get out of control.*

STEVE: What did ya think was gonna happen, mate? How far did ya want it to go? Did ya think Trev and I were gonna lose control or something? Start salivating over her like a couple of dogs on heat. So is this how you two get off, is it? Do ya like watchin' ya girlfriend tease other blokes, do ya? Does it get ya hard, does it mate?

STEVE *puts his arm around* LISA.

Ya know, Lisa, you'd be better off hangin' with me. I'd protect ya. I mean I'd really protect ya. If I saw a couple of thugs slobberin' over you on a train… well, I'd tear their faces off. Why go out with this… bloodless creature? He lives off what's pumpin' through other people's veins.

MAUREEN: Look… I agree with you. They shouldn't have used you but… they've said sorry, so just let them go.

STEVE: Ya reckon that's fair, Maureen? He gets to go home, write his play, and he gets the girl. And what are we left with?

MAUREEN: What you started out with.

STEVE: Exactly. Nothin'!

LISA *starts crying softly.*

See what you've done now, mate.

WRITER: Take your arm off her… please.

STEVE: Come and have a drink with me and Trev, Lisa. I'm upset as well. We've all been used here.

He nuzzles his face into her neck. She recoils.

Jesus, you smell good. You smell like heaven. Can't remember the last time I smelt heaven.

LISA *stands up.*

LISA: [*to the* WRITER] You stupid, stupid… prick! I do not want to be in this situation! Tell me… when exactly were you going to step in and help me? He's right… I feel very fucking used!

STEVE: You tell him, Lisa.

LISA: You can't play with people like this. You told me that everything was going to be under control. Well… it is a long way from that. We're getting off this train now… and I'm going home. [*Turning to*

STEVE] I'll apologise once more. We are so very sorry for this. [*To the* WRITER] Now, let's go.

She makes for the door. STEVE *grabs her, throws her over his shoulder and slams her down onto the seat.*

STEVE: Siddown!

She screams.

Don't side with us just to get your boyfriend off the hook. He doesn't deserve it. You are comin' with us. That's a given.

STEVE *walks towards the* WRITER.

LISA: [*standing up*] Look, let's... have that dance now.

STEVE: Eh?

LISA: You wanted to dance, well... so do I.

He looks her in the eyes and says nothing. He pulls her towards him gently, holding her tight in an intimate embrace. They start moving together. She is shaking uncontrollably. He leads confidently.

STEVE: Tell me, Lisa...

LISA: Yes?

STEVE: Have we made you laugh tonight?

LISA: Yes.

STEVE: You've danced before, haven't you?

LISA: Yes.

STEVE: But you've never caught this train before... have you?

LISA: No.

STEVE: This is the most dangerous thing you've ever done, isn't it?

LISA: Yes.

STEVE: Is it exciting?

LISA: Yes.

STEVE: Is it what you expected?

LISA: No.

STEVE: You're sweating, Lisa.

LISA: There's no air conditioning.

STEVE: Your breath is heavy.

Above: Grant Bowler as Steve and Kirsty Hillhouse as Lisa in the 2002
Perth Theatre Company production. (Photo: Jon Green)
Below: From left: Steve Le Marquand as Steve, Rebecca Massey as Lisa
and Raj Ryan as the Writer in the 2001 Griffin Theatre production in
Sydney. (Photo: Robert McFarlane)

LISA: Is it?

STEVE: Why are you crying?

LISA: I don't know.

STEVE: Do you feel safe in my arms?

LISA: What do you want?

STEVE: What do I want? What do you get for the man who's got fuck-all? How about your phone number for a start?

LISA: I can't.

STEVE: You can't remember your phone number? Must be all the excitement. How about whispering something sweet in my ear?

She doesn't respond.

Whisper something sweet in my ear.

She looks at him, then whispers something. He kisses her. His hand slides over her buttocks and he looks the WRITER *in the eye as he does so.*

[*To the* WRITER] She is magnif—

The WRITER *has pulled a small handgun out of his coat pocket and is resting it on his lap. It is pointing directly at* STEVE.

MAUREEN: Jesus!

Everyone keeps very still. STEVE *glances up at* TREV *then back at the* WRITER *with a smile. He slowly removes his arms from around* LISA *then reaches for the bottle of bourbon and takes a long swig, keeping his eyes locked on the* WRITER *the whole time.*

STEVE: Well, I don't think any of us were expecting this.

WRITER: Come away from him, Lisa.

LISA: Simon…

WRITER: Come… over… here!

She does.

[*To* TREV] Sit down.

He does.

LISA: I was just trying to stop him from—

WRITER: I know.

STEVE: Well, you've officially just become the most dangerous person on this train. No mean feat. Simon, is it?

WRITER: Shut up!

STEVE: All right.

TREV: You're fuckin' dead, mate!

STEVE: Easy, Trev. You wanna… point that thing somewhere else, Simon? You don't look very comfy with it.

WRITER: Most people don't ever go through real pain.

STEVE: 'Scuse me?

WRITER: [*quietly and deliberately*] Most people don't ever go through real pain. They cruise through life in the belief that nothing bad is ever really going to happen to them. Most people don't even think about it until it taps them on the shoulder.

STEVE: What's your point, mate?

WRITER: My point? My point is that… shit always happens to someone else. Someone else's mother or someone else's friend or someone else's brother. Then one day it happens to you and you become the someone else. And all you did was turn your head the wrong way or walk down the wrong lane or step onto the wrong train… [*He looks at* STEVE.] You don't remember my face, do you?

STEVE: Should I?

WRITER: I think you should. Think very hard.

> STEVE *stares at him intensely.*

STEVE: Oh… shit.

TREV: Who is he?

WRITER: Good question, Trevor. Sitting here with a gun on my lap… I'm not sure who I am.

STEVE: Do ya wanna drink?

WRITER: No.

TREV: Who the fuck is he?

WRITER: Tell him.

> *Silence.*

Tell him!

STEVE: Well, I don't know him, but I know who he is. He's the… brother of that guy that attacked me at the nightclub.

TREV: Bullshit!

WRITER: No, he's not bullshitting. At least not about who I am.

STEVE: I didn't recognise you. I remember you wore a hat the whole time
you were in court.

WRITER: It's my brother's hat.

STEVE: I remember thinking it was bad manners at the time.

WRITER: Is that right?

STEVE: You were writin' somethin' in that book then as well… weren't ya?

WRITER: I was writing letters to my brother.

LISA: Simon, what is happening here…?

> *He ignores her.*

WRITER: I was telling him what was happening at the trial. I didn't even
know if he could read it.

STEVE: Yeah… it was a pretty cool hat.

WRITER: What was my brother's name?

STEVE: Um… ah…

WRITER: You don't remember, do you?

> *He points the gun closer.*

It was Dominic.

STEVE: It was comin' to me. Look… Simon, I did my time. Six months
for self defence. I would've got off if I hadn't been on parole already.

WRITER: You are a fucking… liar!

LISA: Simon. Enough. We have to go… now.

STEVE: Simon, my girlfriend witnessed the whole thing. You know that.

WRITER: She is a fucking liar!

> TREV *makes a move towards him.*

Don't… you move any closer to me. Sit down next to him. Now!

STEVE: Look, mate… I understand why you'd be upset, I do… but…

WRITER: You gave him brain damage.

STEVE: Mate…

WRITER: If he could talk, he'd probably tell me to forgive you because
he is a gentle soul. But… he'll never talk again. And… he'll never
hold a lover in his arms again because all he can do now for the rest

of his life is... be held.

ANNOUNCEMENT: *[voice-over] Next station: Mosman Park.*

WRITER: I wish he was dead. And for that reason... for that reason... I cannot forgive you.

TREV: Well, maybe your brother shouldn't have stuck a knife into my mate's leg.

WRITER: You've got everyone believing your little story, haven't you? Dominic... Dominic couldn't even stick a knife into a dead fish.

ANNOUNCEMENT: *[voice-over] Doors closing.*

STEVE: Do you wanna hear this story all over again, do ya? Is that what this is all about? Look... there was one witness. My ex-girlfriend. We were all pissed, it got way outta hand, but your brother started it!

WRITER: How did he start it?

STEVE: Jesus! By gettin' sleazy all over my missus!

WRITER: My brother was gay.

STEVE: Bisexual was the term mentioned at the trial.

WRITER: No... he was gay. Our parents... It killed them when it was brought up at the trial.

MAUREEN: I think you should put that gun away now. This won't help your brother.

WRITER: Do you want to hear the real story, Maureen?

MAUREEN: Why don't you tell me later. Over a couple of beers.

WRITER: Dominic didn't make a move on his girlfriend. Dominic didn't even make a move on him.

STEVE: What the fuck are you talkin'—?

WRITER: I don't know what you said to him. But it was enticing enough to lure him outside into a dark alleyway. I can understand. You're a striking-looking man. You've got a quality that would've excited Dominic a great deal. He would not have been expecting to meet someone like you at a suburban nightclub. He would've thought he was onto a safe bet. And he was pretty pissed. But... you didn't plan for your girlfriend to come out and catch you with your tongue inside another man's mouth... did you? You see... I know how hard it is to come out. My brother couldn't do it. He was in agony over it. But you… you just tried to destroy the evidence. You kicked my brother's head in even after he was screaming for you to stop. And then tried to tell your girlfriend that the poofter on the ground had tried to feel you up. But your girlfriend isn't that stupid… so you threatened her with the same treatment if she went against your story. And you knew you had to have one because that poor poofter on the ground had his blood all over the wall and he wasn't moving.

STEVE: Have you finished with this bullshit?

WRITER: I don't think so.

ANNOUNCEMENT: *[voice-over] Next station: North Fremantle.*

STEVE: So you're not a writer?

WRITER: I am a writer. And I am writing a play. And it will be about you.

STEVE: Why?

WRITER: Writing about you was the only way for me to… take control of the situation.

ANNOUNCEMENT: *[voice-over] Doors closing.*

WRITER: Otherwise I would've gone mad.

STEVE: What ya saying is that you don't have the guts to kill me.

WRITER: I don't know that.

STEVE: So ya write about me?

WRITER: Yes.

STEVE: What'll that do?

WRITER: Damn you to hell forever.

STEVE: So what happens at the end of the play?

WRITER: I don't know yet.

STEVE: What would you like to happen?

WRITER: You die.

STEVE: How?

WRITER: I don't know, but it'll be nasty.

STEVE: Not much for me to get scared about, is there?

WRITER: Yes there is.

STEVE: Why?

WRITER: Because I really, really would like to shoot you. And I'm nervous.

STEVE: You'd have one over me then. I've never shot anybody. I know blokes that have. But they're all living out their lives in a tiny little room with one light bulb and a washbasin. Is that what you want?

WRITER: I'll take my chances!

STEVE: I don't think you're gonna have a choice, mate. See that little camera up there? [*Pointing*] You probably didn't know it was there, did ya? 'Cause I bet you never catch the train. It's Big Brother, mate. Sees everything you do. In a few years you and me are gonna be swappin' prison stories. Whatever ya do… hide your Dencorub.

WRITER: You can shut up now!

STEVE: We're not that different, ya know. We just take our revenge out on the world for different reasons.

WRITER: I'm not taking my revenge out on the world, just you.

STEVE: Ya can't kill me off with words. I've survived everything. I'll be back on this train tomorrow, bigger and stronger than ever. And you'll still be at home [*looking at* LISA] alone, churnin' up inside. Before ya know it, ya hittin' the turps. Hard.

WRITER: Shut up!

STEVE: Or maybe in a particularly desperate moment, you turn the gun onto yourself.

WRITER: *Shut up!*

STEVE: I'm just trying to help you with the ending, Simon.

WRITER: I'm the writer.

STEVE: We're nearly in Freo. Did ya get what ya wanted?

WRITER: Not yet.

STEVE: What did ya want?

> *He points the gun closer.*

WRITER: I want you to tell me what you said to my brother to entice him into the alleyway.

STEVE: How do ya know I said anything?

WRITER: I know. My brother never made the first move.

STEVE: You think ya know ya brother pretty well, don't ya?

WRITER: What did you say to Dominic?!

STEVE: You callin' me a faggot?

WRITER: What did you say to my brother?!

STEVE: It's none of your business!

> *The* WRITER *is shaking now but still holding the gun and his gaze on* STEVE.

WRITER: If you don't tell me what you said before we get to Fremantle, I will shoot you.

> *He points the gun directly at* STEVE's *head.*

STEVE: Fuck off and die!

TREV: Tell him.

STEVE: Eh!

TREV: Tell him.

STEVE: *E tu, Brute?*

TREV: Hey… I woulda taken him out… just like that. But, mate… I know what the deal is in the joint. Sometime stuff just happens. Bad stuff. I know. And I just thought… well… you know, it doesn't matter, 'cause we go back to normal when we get out. But… I don't even remember what normal is anymore. And you know… I don't give a shit. But if you turned his brother into a veggie just 'causa… that, then you gotta tell him. He just wants some peace.

STEVE: No, he doesn't! He wants a confession!

TREV: Just tell him.

STEVE: It's none of his business!

TREV: You been lyin' to me! Haven't ya? Ya fuckin' turd! I don't care who or what ya stick ya dick into. We're both fucked-up units!

STEVE: You're my best friend. Don't you look at me like I'm a condemned man.

TREV: Why don't you grow an extra testicle and tell him what ya said to his brother?! Tell him!

> *He slaps him hard.*

I am just tryin' to save your miserable life just like ya did for me! Tell him or he's gonna kill ya!

STEVE: I don't care.

TREV: There's nowhere to hide anymore… Tell him!

ANNOUNCEMENT: *[voice-over] Next station: Fremantle.*

> *He slaps him harder.*

TREV: *Tell him!*

STEVE: *Sdí ba rúhpa wací! Sdí ba rúhpa wací!*

WRITER: What's he saying?!

STEVE: *[starting to cry as he says it] Sdí ba rúhpa wací!*

> *He turns to look at the* WRITER *and says it defiantly through tears as he slides to the ground.*

TREV: It's Apache. It means: 'The moment of truth between two men'. It's on his tattoo.

> LISA *goes over and puts her hand on* TREV'*s shoulder.*

LISA: Come on. Come and sit down.

TREV: You've never been to Prague... have ya?

LISA: It's a beautiful night outside. I think there's a full moon.

> *The train pulls into the station.*

ANNOUNCEMENT: *[voice-over] This train terminates here.*

LISA: *[to* TREV] Come on. Let's go.

STEVE: Hey... hey! This is Verdi. It's the hundredth anniversary of his death this year. I'd love to be remembered a hundred years after I'm gone. Wouldn't that just be the duck's nuts, eh? I think I'll just stay here and listen.

I was fucking your brother for a whole year. But see, I don't care who I fuck. So when I told him to go away 'cause I was seeing Tanya, he went crazy with a knife. And she saw it outside that nightclub. So he turned on her. He wanted to kill us both. So I stopped him. Your sweet little fucked-up brother. I saved your family from that truth. 'Cause I felt sorry for ya. But I still wake up fuckin' cryin'. He loved me. Understand. He loved me. And he needed me. [*To* LISA] Just like you do. Like ya all do. 'Cause I make you know how lucky and empty your lives are. Put that in your play.

> STEVE *exits. No one moves. The doors open and they all leave at different times, alone.* MAUREEN *is the last to leave. She stops*

when she gets to the door.

ANNOUNCEMENT: *[voice-over] This train runs from Fremantle to Perth stopping all stations. Doors closing.*

She goes back to her original seat then notices the writer's notebook on the seat. She picks it up and flicks to the last couple of pages. She glances over it. The WRITER's *voice drifts in.*

VOICE-OVER: Under the same moon we all staggered in opposite directions. I was wrong. I didn't know this place. This wasn't the place of my childhood. Maybe it never had been. It was dark and I couldn't see it anymore. The only thing I did know was that my brother had loved him. Even more than me. I could almost understand it too…

I'll never see Lisa again. But I know that I'll see him again. On the train again one day. Maybe I'll hold his gaze or maybe we'll just end up staring out different windows…

MAUREEN *drops the notebook and closes her eyes. The light slowly blacks as the sound of a moving train drifts in.*

THE END

www.ingramcontent.com/pod-product-compliance
Lightning Source LLC
Chambersburg PA
CBHW041934090426
42744CB00017B/2060